Published by Creative Education and
Creative Paperbacks
P.O. Box 227, Mankato, Minnesota 56002
Creative Education and Creative Paperbacks
are imprints of The Creative Company
www.thecreativecompany.us

Design by The Design Lab
Production by Chelsey Luther
Art direction by Rita Marshall
Printed in the United States of America

Photographs by Alamy (Arco Images GmbH, Chris
Godfrey Wildlife Photography, Kenneth Dear, FLPA,
Janette Hill), Dreamstime (KMWphotography),
FreeVectorMaps.com, Getty Images (Kathleen Reeder
Wildlife Photography, Frank Pali), iStockphoto
(abzerit), Shutterstock (Dennis W Donohue, Alan
Jeffery, Abeselom Zerit)

Library of Congress Cataloging-in-Publication Data
Names: Bodden, Valerie.
Title: Snow leopards / Valerie Bodden.
Series: Amazing Animals.
Includes bibliographical references and index.
Summary: A basic exploration of the appearance,
behavior, and habitat of snow leopards, the non-
roaring big cats of Central Asia. Also included is a
story from folklore explaining why snow leopards
have spotted fur.
Identifiers: ISBN 978-1-60818-884-0 (hardcover)
/ ISBN 978-1-62832-500-3 (pbk) / ISBN 978-1-
56660-936-4 (eBook)

This title has been submitted for CIP processing under
LCCN 2017937607.

CCSS: RI.1.1, 2, 4, 5, 6, 7; RI.2.2, 5, 6, 7, 10;
RI.3.1, 5, 7, 8; RF.1.1, 3, 4; RF.2.3, 4

First Edition HC 9 8 7 6 5 4 3 2 1
First Edition PBK 9 8 7 6 5 4 3 2 1

AMAZING ANIMALS

SNOW LEOPARDS

BY VALERIE BODDEN

CREATIVE EDUCATION • CREATIVE PAPERBACKS

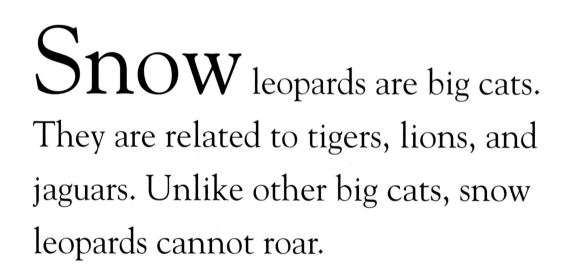

Snow leopards are big cats. They are related to tigers, lions, and jaguars. Unlike other big cats, snow leopards cannot roar.

Thick fur keeps snow leopards warm in cold, snowy weather

Snow leopards have thick fur. It can be white, gray, or light yellow. Black or gray spots called rosettes (*ro-ZETS*) dot the fur. A snow leopard's long, thick tail helps it balance. Big feet help snow leopards walk on top of snow.

No two snow leopards have the same pattern of rosettes

Most snow leopards measure 3 to 4.8 feet (0.9–1.5 m) from front to back. The big cats weigh up to 120 pounds (54.4 kg). Snow leopards can jump 30 feet (9.1 m) at once!

A snow leopard's thick tail can be as long as its body

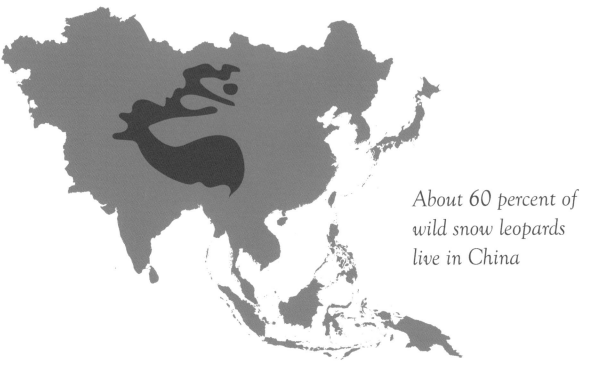

About 60 percent of wild snow leopards live in China

Snow leopards live in Central Asia. Some of the highest **mountains** in the world are there. They are steep and rocky. Snow covers the ground most of the year.

mountains very big hills made of rock

Large paws act as snowshoes, keeping the big cat on top of snow

Snow leopards are **predators**. Their favorite **prey** are wild sheep and wild goats called ibex (*I-beks*). They eat smaller animals such as **marmots**, mice, and birds. Sometimes they also eat grass.

marmots rodents with short legs and short, thick tails

predators animals that kill and eat other animals

prey animals that are killed and eaten by other animals

A cub's bright blue
eyes become pale gray
or green as it ages

A mother snow leopard gives birth to two or three **cubs** in a **den**. The cubs drink milk from their mother. At three months old, they learn how to hunt. They stay with their mother for almost two years. Most wild snow leopards live 10 to 15 years.

cubs baby snow leopards

den a home that is hidden, like a cave

Snow leopards live alone. They are most active in the morning and at night. They walk around searching for prey. When they find a prey animal, they jump on it from above.

Long tails help snow leopards leap accurately

Snow leopards sleep a lot. They may sleep 12 to 20 hours a day. They curl their tail over their nose to stay warm.

Like other cats, snow leopards often yawn when content

Snow leopards are hard to spot in the wild. But many people visit them in zoos. It can be fun to watch these big cats in action!

About 600 snow leopards live in zoos around the world

A Snow Leopard Story

Why do snow leopards have spotted fur? People in Siberia told a story about this. Once there was a princess who wanted to marry a man she met in the mountains. He wore a white fur cloak. One day, the princess found the man's cloak. It was spotted with muddy horse hoof prints. The princess put the cloak on. Instantly, she became a snow leopard.

Read More

Borgert-Spaniol, Megan. *Snow Leopards*. Minneapolis: Bellwether Media, 2014.

West, David. *Mountain Animals*. Chicago: Bright Connections Media, 2015.

Websites

Enchanted Learning: Snow Leopard
http://www.enchantedlearning.com/subjects/mammals/cats/leopard/Snowleopardprintout.shtml
This site has snow leopard facts and a picture to color.

San Diego Zoo Kids: Snow Leopard
http://kids.sandiegozoo.org/animals/mammals/snow-leopard
Learn more about snow leopards.

Note: Every effort has been made to ensure that the websites listed above are suitable for children, that they have educational value, and that they contain no inappropriate material. However, because of the nature of the Internet, it is impossible to guarantee that these sites will remain active indefinitely or that their contents will not be altered.

Index